Francis Frith's
REDHILL TO REIGATE

PHOTOGRAPHIC MEMORIES

Francis Frith's
REDHILL TO REIGATE

◆

Dennis Needham

THE FRANCIS FRITH COLLECTION

FRITH
BOOK Co

First published in the United Kingdom in 2000 by
Frith Book Company Ltd

Hardback Edition 2000
ISBN 1-85937-137-x

Paperback Edition 2002
ISBN 1-85937-596-0

British Library Cataloguing in Publication Data

Francis Frith's Redhill to Reigate
Dennis Needham
Additional research by Jac Mason and Nigel Needham

Frith Book Company Ltd
Frith's Barn, Teffont,
Salisbury, Wiltshire SP3 5QP
Tel: +44 (0) 1722 716 376
Email: info@francisfrith.co.uk
www.francisfrith.co.uk

Printed and bound in Great Britain

AS WITH ANY HISTORICAL DATABASE THE FRITH ARCHIVE IS CONSTANTLY BEING CORRECTED AND IMPROVED
AND THE PUBLISHERS WOULD WELCOME INFORMATION ON OMISSIONS OR INACCURACIES

Contents

◆

FRANCIS FRITH: *Victorian Pioneer*

FRANCIS FRITH, Victorian founder of the world-famous photographic archive, was a complex and fascinating man. A devout Quaker and a highly successful Victorian businessman, he was both philosophic by nature and pioneering in outlook.

By 1855 Francis Frith had already established a wholesale grocery business in Liverpool, and sold it for the astonishing sum of £200,000, which is the equivalent today of over £15,000,000. Now a multi-millionaire, he was able to indulge his passion for travel. As a child he had pored over travel books written by early explorers, and his fancy and imagination had been stirred by family holidays to the sublime mountain regions of Wales and Scotland. 'What a land of spirit-stirring and enriching scenes and places!' he had written. He was to return to these scenes of grandeur in later years to 'recapture the thousands of vivid and tender memories', but with a different purpose. Now in his thirties, and captivated by the new science of photography, Frith set out on a series of pioneering journeys to the Nile regions that occupied him from 1856 until 1860.

INTRIGUE AND ADVENTURE

He took with him on his travels a specially-designed wicker carriage that acted as both dark-room and sleeping chamber. These far-flung journeys were packed with intrigue and adventure. In his life story, written when he was sixty-three, Frith tells of being held captive by bandits, and of fighting 'an awful midnight battle to the very point of surrender with a deadly pack of hungry, wild dogs'. Sporting flowing Arab costume, Frith arrived at Akaba by camel seventy years before Lawrence, where he encountered 'desert princes and rival sheikhs, blazing with jewel-hilted swords'.

During these extraordinary adventures he was assiduously exploring the desert regions bordering the Nile and patiently recording the antiquities and peoples with his camera. He was the first photographer to venture beyond the sixth cataract. Africa was still the mysterious 'Dark Continent', and Stanley and Livingstone's historic meeting was a decade into the future. The conditions for picture taking confound belief. He laboured for hours in his wicker dark-room in the sweltering heat of the desert, while the volatile chemicals fizzed dangerously in their trays. Often he was forced to work in remote tombs and caves where conditions were cooler. Back in London he exhibited his photographs and was 'rapturously cheered' by members of the Royal Society. His reputation as a photographer was made overnight. An eminent modern historian has likened their impact on the population of the time to that on our own generation of the first photographs taken on the surface of the moon.

VENTURE OF A LIFE-TIME

Characteristically, Frith quickly spotted the opportunity to create a new business as a specialist publisher of photographs. He lived in an era of immense and sometimes violent change. For the poor in the early part of Victoria's reign work was a drudge and the hours long, and people had precious little free time to enjoy themselves.

Most had no transport other than a cart or gig at their disposal, and had not travelled far beyond the boundaries of their own town or village. However, by the 1870s, the railways had threaded their way across the country, and Bank Holidays and half-day Saturdays had been made obligatory by Act of Parliament. All of a sudden the ordinary working man and his family were able to enjoy days out and see a little more of the world.

With characteristic business acumen, Francis Frith foresaw that these new tourists would enjoy having souvenirs to commemorate their days out. In 1860 he married Mary Ann Rosling of Reigate and formed F Frith & Co Ltd, with the intention of photographing every city, town and village in Britain. For the next thirty years he travelled the country by train and by pony and trap, producing fine photographs of seaside resorts and beauty spots that were keenly bought by millions of Victorians. These prints were painstakingly pasted into family albums and pored over during the dark nights of winter, rekindling precious memories of summer excursions.

THE RISE OF FRITH & CO

Frith's studio was soon supplying retail shops all over the country. To meet the demand he gathered about him a small team of photographers, and published the work of independent artist-photographers of the calibre of Roger Fenton and Francis Bedford. In order to gain some understanding of the scale of Frith's business one only has to look at the catalogue issued by

Frith & Co in 1886: it runs to some 670 pages, listing not only many thousands of views of the British Isles but also many photographs of most European countries, and China, Japan, the USA and Canada – note the sample page shown above from the hand-written *Frith & Co* ledgers detailing pictures taken. By 1890 Frith had created the greatest specialist photographic publishing company in the world, with over 2,000 outlets – more than the combined number that Boots and WH Smith have today! The picture on the right shows the *Frith & Co* display board at Ingleton in the Yorkshire Dales. Beautifully constructed with mahogany frame and gilt inserts, it could display up to a dozen local scenes.

POSTCARD BONANZA

The ever-popular holiday postcard we know today took many years to develop. In 1870 the Post Office issued the first plain cards, with a pre-printed stamp on one face. In 1894 they allowed other publishers' cards to be sent through the mail with an attached adhesive halfpenny stamp. Demand grew rapidly, and in 1895 a new

size of postcard was permitted called the court card, but there was little room for illustration. In 1899, a year after Frith's death, a new card measuring 5.5 x 3.5 inches became the standard format, but it was not until 1902 that the divided back came into being, with address and message on one face and a full-size illustration on the other. *Frith & Co* were in the vanguard of postcard development, and Frith's sons Eustace and Cyril continued their father's monumental task, expanding the number of views offered to the public and recording more and more places in Britain, as the coasts and countryside were opened up to mass travel.

Francis Frith died in 1898 at his villa in Cannes, his great project still growing. The archive he created continued in business for another seventy years. By 1970 it contained over a third of a million pictures of 7,000 cities, towns and villages. The massive photographic record Frith has left to us stands as a living monument to a special and very remarkable man.

Frith's Archive: *A Unique Legacy*

FRANCIS FRITH'S legacy to us today is of immense significance and value, for the magnificent archive of evocative photographs he created provides a unique record of change in 7,000 cities, towns and villages throughout Britain over a century and more. Frith and his fellow studio photographers revisited locations many times down the years to update their views, compiling for us an enthralling and colourful pageant of British life and character.

We tend to think of Frith's sepia views of Britain as nostalgic, for most of us use them to conjure up memories of places in our own lives with which we have family associations. It often makes us forget that to Francis Frith they were records of daily life as it was actually being lived in the cities, towns and villages of his day. The Victorian age was one of great and often bewildering change for ordinary people, and though the pictures evoke an impression of slower times, life was as busy and hectic as it is today.

We are fortunate that Frith was a photographer of the people, dedicated to recording the minutiae of everyday life. For it is this sheer wealth of visual data, the painstaking chronicle of changes in dress, transport, street layouts, buildings, housing, engineering and landscape that captivates us so much today. His remarkable images offer us a powerful link with the past and with the lives of our ancestors.

TODAY'S TECHNOLOGY

Computers have now made it possible for Frith's many thousands of images to be accessed almost instantly. In the Frith archive today, each photograph is carefully 'digitised' then stored on a CD Rom. Frith archivists can locate a single photograph amongst thousands within seconds. Views can be catalogued and sorted under a variety of categories of place and content to the immediate benefit of researchers. Inexpensive reference prints can be created for them at the touch of a mouse button, and a wide range of books and other printed materials assembled and published for a wider, more general readership - in the next twelve months over a hundred Frith local history titles will be published! The

See Frith at www.francisfrith.co.uk

day-to-day workings of the archive are very different from how they were in Francis Frith's time: imagine the herculean task of sorting through eleven tons of glass negatives as Frith had to do to locate a particular sequence of pictures! Yet the archive still prides itself on maintaining the same high standards of excellence laid down by Francis Frith, including the painstaking cataloguing and indexing of every view.

It is curious to reflect on how the internet now allows researchers in America and elsewhere greater instant access to the archive than Frith himself ever enjoyed. Many thousands of individual views can be called up on screen within seconds on one of the Frith internet sites, enabling people living continents away to revisit the streets of their ancestral home town, or view places in Britain where they have enjoyed holidays. Many overseas researchers welcome the chance to view special theme selections, such as transport, sports, costume and ancient monuments.

We are certain that Francis Frith would have heartily approved of these modern developments, for he himself was always working at the very limits of Victorian photographic technology.

The Value of the Archive Today

Because of the benefits brought by the computer, Frith's images are increasingly studied by social historians, by researchers into genealogy and ancestry, by architects, town planners, and by teachers and schoolchildren involved in local history projects. In addition, the archive offers every one of us a unique opportunity to examine the places where we and our families have lived and worked down the years. Immensely successful in Frith's own era, the archive is now, a century and more on, entering a new phase of popularity.

The Past in Tune with the Future

Historians consider the Francis Frith Collection to be of prime national importance. It is the only archive of its kind remaining in private ownership and has been valued at a million pounds. However, this figure is now rapidly increasing as digital technology enables more and more people around the world to enjoy its benefits.

Francis Frith's archive is now housed in an historic timber barn in the beautiful village of Teffont in Wiltshire. Its founder would not recognize the archive office as it is today. In place of the many thousands of dusty boxes containing glass plate negatives and an all-pervading odour of photographic chemicals, there are now ranks of computer screens. He would be amazed to watch his images travelling round the world at unimaginable speeds through network and internet lines.

The archive's future is both bright and exciting. Francis Frith, with his unshakeable belief in making photographs available to the greatest number of people, would undoubtedly approve of what is being done today with his lifetime's work. His photographs, depicting our shared past, are now bringing pleasure and enlightenment to millions around the world a century and more after his death.

REDHILL TO REIGATE
An Introduction

REIGATE AND REDHILL are inextricably joined together by ever-expanding commuter housing, but they are as different as chalk and cheese.

Redhill is the upstart newcomer. In the early years of the 19th century, the town simply did not exist, for it was nothing more than a boggy wasteland. There were a few houses on the northern edge of what is now Earlswood Common, and some others to the north of Redhill town centre. By assiduously searching, some of the other 17th- and 18th-century houses can still be found. In 1818 a road was constructed through what we now know as Redhill, and the men working on that road needed somewhere to live. Then, in 1841, the London and Brighton Railway came through. The navvies working on that also needed accommodation. Thus were the foundations of the town laid.

If the road was important, the railway was crucial, although it might not have been quite so important had it not been for two facts. First, Redstone Hill (as it was then known) was roughly halfway between London and Brighton, making it a convenient place for the steam locomotives to take on water. Refuelling facilities were also provided at an engine shed. Then, the South East Railway opened their line along the foot of the Downs; this ran from Folkestone to a terminus close to the L & B line at Redstone Hill. By 1844, the foolishness of this situation was recognised by both companies, and the lines were connected. The original L & B station had been further to the south, so this was closed, and a new one, known as Reigate, was opened. Over the years, this would become Reigate Junction, Red Hill Junction and eventually Redhill.

Whilst the initial development had taken place to the south of the centre in an area known as St Johns, re-locating the station half a mile to the north had, along with the proximity of the road, seen a drift to the north. This part of Surrey would become known as Warwick Town after the Countess of Warwick, who had provided her land here for house-building. Within a few years, the district had started to develop into what it is today: a commuter town.

The name of Redhill was not long in coming. A local post office was opened in Station Road, the second in the area, both of which were sub-offices of the main (Reigate) one. So that they could be identified separately for the purposes of forwarding mail, the name Red Hill was adopted. This was the principal reason for the demise of Warwick Town; the name was simply adopted by local businesses who were users of the mail.

Before long, a railway was opened from Redhill station to Reading, and Reigate got its own station. This speeded up the process of each place having its own identity, but in subsequent years, as has been already mentioned, building had filled in the gaps between the two places. As the town developed its fast and frequent train services to London, more and more people recognised the two towns as great places to live whilst still being within easy reach of London. Every working day, thousands of commuters leave the area through Redhill station; both towns have grown at a phenomenal rate. Redhill has developed into a thriving and bustling commercial centre with the best range of large stores. This extensive range of shops and facilities draws people from a large area. As commuters leave, their wives invade the supermarkets and stores.

Since Redhill is a relatively recent creation, nearly all the building is modern. It is almost as though the first surge of development all became life-expired at around the same time; a massive rebuilding programme in post-war years has created much that is architecturally suspect, albeit thoroughly functional.

But history did come to the town. In 1896, a law was repealed, the one that demanded that a man walk in front of a car with a red flag. To celebrate, a group of motorists organ-

Redhill, Station Road East 1906 55033

ised a run from London to Brighton in celebration. The original route would have bypassed Redhill, but at the last minute cars were re-routed through the town, travelling down London Road and turning right into Station Road to reach Reigate. Every year now, the event is recreated by the RAC, who organise their event on the first Sunday in November. Hundreds of these lovely old

lished. The Dissolution of the Monasteries began in 1536, and Reigate was an early victim. The king expropriated all the land and assets of the monasteries, and installed Lord Edmund Howard to manage the priory. Shortly afterwards the king died. His daughter became queen, and her uncle, William Howard, became the priory's owner. From then on, it would become a private house, a

Reigate, High Street 1919 68894

machines leave London from 7.30am, and the first will reach Reigate an hour later.

Yet Reigate is anything but the staid old town it once was. The history of the town goes back to beyond Domesday. But it was the establishment of an Augustinian Priory that saw the development of Reigate. This took place around 1230. For the next three centuries, the area grew steadily as the priory prospered. But then Henry VIII fell out with Rome and the Church of England was estab-

function it retained until the start of the last war. It suffered some neglect during the hostilities but in 1948, after refurbishment, it became a school, a purpose it serves to this day.

With ownership of the priory went ownership of much of the town. That situation was to change abruptly in 1921 when the town went on sale. This singular event brought massive interest and subsequently became known as The Great Sale of Reigate.

Hundreds of local people bought their own shops, hotels, businesses and homes. Suddenly, the town was liberated. Whether or not that turned out to be a good thing is still debated in the town. Over the next two decades, wholesale reconstruction took place. Dozens of fine Georgian buildings were razed in a frenzy of 'modernisation'. What took their place was questionable at best. But all was far from lost. Enough people created enough fuss, and gradually Reigate regained its sanity. We are most fortunate today that this happened. To wander around the town is almost to enter a time-warp. There is so much to see and enjoy, a process that will, we hope, be aided by this volume.

Having already seen how much both road and rail were to influence the development of this area, it is only fitting that the next major development on the travel front should also affect the towns. Gatwick Airport started life as an airfield in 1936; it was taken over by the Air Ministry, who set up a flying school there the following year. It was used by the RAF during the hostilities, and was returned to civilian use afterwards. In 1956 it closed for extensive rebuilding, re-opening as London Gatwick - London's second international airport - in 1958. Since then it has just continued to grow. Many people from both Redhill and Reigate work there, both as ground support and aircrew. Not all commuter traffic goes north. With a main line railway station there, it is easy to reach from Redhill station. Gatwick also has a superb non-stop service to London every fifteen minutes.

Considering its status as a commuter town, there is a remarkable amount of 'green' around the periphery of both Redhill and Reigate. Nestling as they do in the soft under-belly of the North Downs, there is plenty of chalk upland to explore north of the towns. Colley Hill, Reigate Hill, Gatton Park, Serpentine Wood - all these have grass and trees in plenty, criss-crossed by a large number of tracks and public footpaths. But the area does have one blight. Cutting a swathe through this beautiful area is the M25, that most obnoxious of motorways. Its noise pollution affects large tracts of this otherwise peaceful upland. There are similar areas to walk in, relax in and enjoy south of the towns. But do not go too far south. There, noise from Gatwick can become a problem.

But it is not all bad. There are some delicate leafy corners both in and out of town to find, explore and enjoy. One of the great pleasures of jaunts such as this is to carry this volume along with you. Enjoy the experience of working out just where our photographer set up his equipment all those years ago. As you snap away at the same view with your automatic camera, picture the back-breaking load of gear those pioneers carried. Marvel at how little our green and pleasant land has changed during the intervening years. Or perhaps frown at the wanton destruction of eye-pleasing views and try to decide how such architectural nightmares that sometimes stand in their place ever came to be built. Wonder at the acres of green fields that have disappeared under a welter of bricks and concrete.

This is a book for all seasons. Muse over it from your armchair during the long winter months. Then travel into Surrey during the more pleasant summer days. But, above all, enjoy the sheer pleasure of nostalgia as displayed within these covers.

REIGATE, THE SUSPENSION BRIDGE 1886 18968A
This gorgeous bridge is now no more, replaced by a concrete crossing. The North Downs Way, a 140-mile path from Farnham (Surrey) to Dover crosses here. This busy scene has observers on the bridge, a cyclist and two coaches - the second one is largely concealed behind the leading horses.

REIGATE, OVERLOOKING THE TOWN 1906 54133A

When this view overlooking Reigate was taken, there was little in the way of development. Now, it is wall-to-wall housing. The housing to the left still exists, and the hillside in the picture, now owned by the National Trust, is a popular local beauty spot complete with its own café.

REIGATE, THE YEW TREE AND REIGATE HILL c1955 R20043

A pastoral scene of half a century ago has changed little. The pub still flourishes - although it does not advertise mineral waters any more - and the street lighting has changed.

REIGATE, THE MUNICIPAL BUILDINGS c1965 R20206
This view indicates the sea-change that has taken place in our motor industry. With one exception, everything is from the BMC/British Leyland stable - Austin and Morris, both medium saloons, minis, 1100s and the Morris Minor. Today, to all intents and purposes, the whole lot is extinct.

REIGATE, WEST STREET 1886 18958
West Street is now the A25 road towards Dorking. In this view, it is still unsurfaced, although the footpath has been raised and kerbstones fitted. The large house in the right-hand distance now carries a blue plaque noting that it is of historic interest.

REIGATE, WEST STREET 1906 54149

Here we see a beautiful portrait of England as it once was. The gorgeous spreading trees, the horse and cart - it is hard to believe that this is the A25 trunk road today. Needless to say, it has been widened and altered beyond recognition.

REIGATE, NUTLEY LANE 1906 54739

Looking away from the centre of town, on the right is The Beehive General Store, now gone the way of most suburban shops of this nature: it has been converted to a house. The shop on the left still exists; it is now a violin workshop.

REIGATE, SOMERS ROAD 1908 60285
Flourishing trees dominate this view of Somers Road. Take away the tradesman with his horse and cart and the gentleman on the pavement opposite and surface the road, and you have a perfect, timeless picture of suburbia.

REIGATE, LONDON ROAD C1965 R20240
This view looks north in an area that has seen remarkable change in recent years. The long low building in front of the Railway Hotel (middle distance) is a signal cabin for the railway. That is still there, but even the approach to the station has changed.

REIGATE, SOUTH PARK CONVALESCENT HOME 1891 29582A
A favoured way of recovering from illness, the convalescent home has reduced in significance with the subsequent improvement in medical care. This place still exists, as The Margaret Laurie Day Hospital. Notice the ladies and gentlemen ruthlessly separated, with nurses between.

REIGATE
Park Lane 1906 54148

This is a fascinating study of life a hundred years ago with all the characters carefully posed. The butchers to the left was established in 1813, but it has not survived today. The white house (centre) carries the slogan 'Peace Proclaimed June 1903': which peace? The cart in the distance is delivering coal.

REIGATE, WESTERN PARADE c1955 R20062
This is now a major road junction where Prices Lane (in the foreground) meets Cockshot Hill. The ancient road sign demanding a 'Slow' would scarcely suffice for today's traffic. The building to the right is The Angel pub, which has now lost its trees.

REIGATE, CORNFIELD ROAD 1906 56205
This 19th-century housing estate survives largely intact. Note the complete lack of people save the two youngsters. The house on the left now carries a blue plaque informing us (erroneously) that Oscar Wilde lived here once.

REIGATE
Cornfield Road 1910 62762
Four short years after photograph No
56205, the pavements have been
separated from the road, but no metalled
surface has yet been applied. The steps
and shop (left) survive, but it is now
selling soft furnishings. Many of the
products emblazoned in the windows are
still available today. It is quite remarkable
that an area such as this could support
two almost identical shops.

REIGATE
Cockshot Road 1910 62764
Cornfield Road bakery on the junction with Cornfield
Road can be seen right of centre. Perambulators,
parasols and handcarts, perhaps the leitmotif of
Edwardian England, are well in evidence.

REIGATE, SPRINGCOPSE ROAD 1906 56206
Running parallel with Cornfield Road, Springcopse Road was developed at the same time. The elegant iron railings of the houses to the left are no more: they were probably removed for the production of munitions in the war.

REIGATE, THE RED CROSS c1955 R20091
This is a fine example of a brewery's vandalism. There has been a pub called The Red Cross (main building on the right) on this site since the mid 1500s. Today, it is called the Tap and Spile, a name treated with scorn by most locals.

REIGATE, WRAY LANE 1906 54593
This narrow little lane has changed little in the intervening years. The house has a hedge of conifers in front of it, and the road surface is much improved. The lady with her perambulator in the yard to the low side of the houses is clearly enjoying the fine weather.

The Windmill 1893
Although looking in an advanced state of decay, this windmill was probably still working at the time of the picture. It is a crown type of mill: the upper tower revolves so that the sails are square to the wind. The other type - a post mill - has the whole body of the mill revolving. The grain store alongside would be raised from the ground to aid ventilation and protect from vermin.

REIGATE
Wray Common Windmill 1907
A further view of the windmill, now clearly in an advanced state of disrepair. Today, the sails are gone and the body of the mill is part of a house.

REIGATE, THE WINDMILL 1893 33231

REIGATE, WRAY COMMON WINDMILL 1907 59254

REIGATE, THE CASTLE GROUNDS 1915 67779
Here we see Reigate at ease during the first world war. It is noticeable that there are no men at all in this view. The Grounds were opened to the public in the mid 19th century by the third Earl Somers.

REIGATE, THE PARK 1894 34160
This is a wonderful view of Reigate Park, with two young ladies carefully positioned by the cameraman and holding very still. Saying 'cheese' to the camera was seemingly not practised in those days.

REIGATE
The Pageant 1913 R20304
This is Colley Hill. The occasion was a celebration of
the acquisition of this land by the National Trust. The
wonderful top-hatted figure is Lord Curzon; at the
time he was in the political wilderness. He resigned as
Viceroy of India in 1905, and was not appointed to the
war cabinet until 1916. He was a most
able politician.

REIGATE, THE WINDMILL c1965 R20214

This post windmill is on Reigate Heath. Reigate Mill is believed to have been built in the 1760s, and was grinding corn for a century until 1768. In 1880 the roundhouse was converted and became the St John Cross Chapel - there was once a chantry chapel of the Holy Cross in the High Street opposite the Red Cross Inn. The sails of the mill were damaged by gales in 1999, and have since been replaced as part of a restoration scheme.

REIGATE, BUCKLAND SCHOOLS 1891 29583

The village of Buckland is a few miles west of Reigate on the A25. Before the advent of the motor vehicle, it was a quiet remote place. Now the main road thunders through. The school to the left is now a private house, and a war memorial can be found alongside the pond.

REIGATE, RICEBRIDGE, ON THE MOLE 1886 18821
Ricebridge is to the south-west of Reigate; to this day, a footbridge spans the river here. The Mole rises deep in Sussex and empties into the river Thames opposite Hampton Court.

REIGATE
Vanderbilt's Coach 'Venture' c1908 18968B
During the revival period of coaching, the American millionaire Alfred G. Vanderbilt ran his *'Venture'* coach on the London-Brighton road during the summer seasons of 1908 to the outbreak of war in 1914, with a second coach, the *'Viking'*, in 1909. The *'Venture'* is seen here climbing the steep Reigate Hill with the aid of an extra pair of horses, one of them ridden by a "post boy" in his fine livery. Following the coach is a more modest American carriage, with a local delivery driver watching them pass.

REIGATE, HIGH STREET 1886 18956

A rutted, filthy road is the main thing to notice here, along with a complete lack of vehicles. The Methodist Church, still there today, is the only building to have gas-fuelled street lights outside.

REIGATE, HIGH STREET 1911 63190

Street lamps are now common currency, and cycles have made their appearance. The shop on the left is a photographer's, but seemingly not part of Frith's company which continued to have connections with Reigate until 1970.

REIGATE, HIGH STREET 1919 68894
It is eight years after photograph No 63190, and the town is getting busier. The building beyond the cars is the White Hart. It is now a Barclays Bank, as will be seen later. Electricity has replaced gas for the street lighting.

REIGATE
High Street 1919 68895
A view from the west end looking towards town. The
omnibus approaching the camera seems alarmingly
top-heavy. The newsagent's shop, left, has a billboard
outside proclaiming 'More troops for Ireland'.
80 years along, nothing has changed.

REIGATE, HIGH STREET c1955 R20067

Now we are in post-war times, and the motor-car has really taken over. Several of the businesses that can be seen in this view are no more. A driving school and the almost inevitable building society are just a couple that have taken over some of the premises. The White Hart has now become Barclays.

REIGATE, HIGH STREET c1955 R20068

The elegant shop front of A Jones & Sons survives to this day, but the white-fronted shop is no more. The Old Town Hall clock continues to give the time to the residents of the town, as it has done for years now.

REIGATE
High Street c 1965

By the 1960s, a zebra crossing defaces the street surface. The first signs of the foreign car invasions can be seen: a Renault approaches the camera. In front of the Old Market Hall - built in 1720 - is a telephone box. Today, this is still a red one rather than the shiny new BT monstrosity.

◆

REIGATE
High Street c1965

This view looks west along the High Street from the upper window of the Old Town Hall. On the left, the Westminster Bank has become the Natwest; Timothy Whites and Woolworth's no longer occupy those premises. Old-fashioned sun blinds are very much in evidence on the shops to the right.

REIGATE, HIGH STREET C 1965   R20188

REIGATE, HIGH STREET c1965   R20103

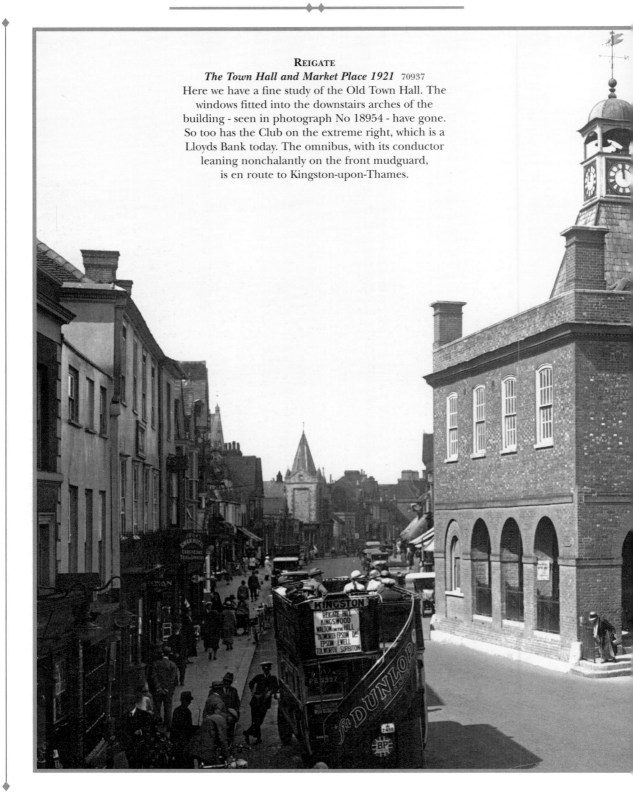

REIGATE

The Town Hall and Market Place 1921 70937

Here we have a fine study of the Old Town Hall. The
windows fitted into the downstairs arches of the
building - seen in photograph No 18954 - have gone.
So too has the Club on the extreme right, which is a
Lloyds Bank today. The omnibus, with its conductor
leaning nonchalantly on the front mudguard,
is en route to Kingston-upon-Thames.

REIGATE, MARKET PLACE 1896 18954
An early morning view of the Old Town Hall, built in the 18th century. Note the chimneys on each corner: only one had a fire beneath it, while the others were for aesthetic appeal. The shop windows to the left are archetypal Victorian ones, but are now history. Together with The Swan, they were demolished around 1935.

REIGATE, THE TOWN CENTRE 1939 88864
By 1930, the White Hart pub on the left corner had been replaced by a Barclays bank. To the right of the market square, the Crown Hotel has been re-named The Market Hotel: this just proves that today's obsession with changing old pub names is not new.

REIGATE, MARKET PLACE AND HIGH STREET 1939 88865

The buildings that have replaced the old, as seen in the two older views taken from this location, are now in place. On the extreme left, Dunsford's has become a menswear shop and Burtons, then part of a huge chain of retail menswear shops, has changed into a bed store. It is sad that the delightfully ornate direction sign is no more.

REIGATE, CHURCH STREET 1909 61639

Church Street brings the A25 into town from the east. Note that everyone in the picture is wearing a hat of some description. The two ladies on the cart leaving town have the additional protection of a parasol. Everything has changed here; shops and flats line the road today.

REIGATE, CHURCH STREET c1955   R20007

REIGATE
Church Street c1955

Just how much the road has changed can be gleaned from this picture. Compare it with photograph No 61639 and marvel at what changes half a century can wreak. Note the undeveloped land further up on the right. But it will not remain undeveloped for long.

◆

REIGATE
Church Street c1965

It is ten short years after photograph No R20007, and that undeveloped space has gone, infilled by more shops and flats. This view, taken from the upstairs rooms of the Old Wheel Tea Room, allows a view over the rooftops. The number of aerials to be seen is staggering.

REIGATE, CHURCH STREET c1965   R20207

REIGATE, CHURCH STREET c1965 R20136
This is a similar view to photograph No R20207, but it concentrates much more on the traffic. A Renault Dauphine is parked to the extreme right, and the second-last car moving is an Austin A40 being used as a driving school vehicle.

REIGATE, CHURCH STREET c1965 R20137
What is revealing about this view is the number of Morris Minor cars in shot: no less than five! There are two delivery trucks, an Austin on the left delivering Cadbury's chocolate, and an Albion on the right with Jacobs biscuits. Whilst the products still exist, the delivery system today relies on supermarkets or cash-and-carry.

REIGATE, CHURCH STREET c1965 R20189
The Tesco Food Fair on the left is still the same building today, but the Café Rouge occupies the ground floor. The view today is instantly recognisable.

REIGATE, BELL STREET 1908 61153
From the centre of town, the southbound road is the A217 to Crawley; Bell Street. This view - and the next half dozen - will all look towards the town centre during a span of a number of years. Note the young trees on the left, their trunks protected by iron fencing.

REIGATE, BELL STREET 1936 87306

It is thirty years after photograph No 61153, taken from an identical viewpoint. The trees have grown well, the building to the right has lost its nearest gable and the shop window has been completely rebuilt. This was to allow the garage company access to land they had bought.

REIGATE, BELL STREET c1955 R20041

The ironwork arch of the garage has gone, and new shops have been built (right). The huge Ancient Bookshop sign seen in the last view has also gone. It was new then and it did not last long: it blew down. This splendid emporium still trades to this day.

REIGATE
Bell Street c1955 R20021
Pre-war cars still dominate this view, with a particularly attractive Riley outside the Reigate Garage premises. There is still a hairdresser's in the building on the extreme right, together with a surveyor's.

REIGATE
Bell Street c1955
Everything on the left of this view has been destroyed to make way for a Safeway supermarket. The cinema on the right is a car showroom, although a cinema does still exist in town. The petrol pumps clearly belong to another era.

◆

REIGATE
Bell Street c1955
Note the building on the left with a series of Union Jacks flying. To the right, selling radios is clearly still a profitable line: today it would be TVs or computers.

REIGATE, BELL STREET C1955 R20022

REIGATE, BELL STREET C1955 R20601

REIGATE, BELL STREET c1965 R20237
In the middle distance, directly behind the banner, is an area of black. This is a footpath through a tunnel. This was the road into town from the north until modern traffic conditions rendered it useless. It was cut in 1823, and was the first road tunnel in England.

REIGATE, BELL STREET c1965 R20101
This view back down Bell Street looks towards the camera location for the previous shots. The edge of Barclays bank can be seen on the left, and the National Provincial Bank on the right has yet to become the Natwest.

REIGATE, THE PARISH CHURCH AND THE LYCHGATE 1908 60285A
St Mary Magdalene is one of the largest parish churches in Surrey. The nave is late 12th-century, and the tower was rebuilt in the 19th century. In the vaults lie the mortal remains of Lord Howard of Effingham; he was the Commander-in-Chief of the English fleet which defeated the Spanish Armada.

REDHILL, ST MATTHEW'S CHURCH 1919 68886
Opposite the church today are the offices of the car manufacturer Toyota, who produce altogether more bland (although more comfortable) cars than the one illustrated. The church itself, which was only consecrated in 1866, is built of local Reigate stone.

REDHILL, SHAW'S CORNER 1924 75199

REDHILL
Shaw's Corner 1924
St Paul's was built as a Presbyterian church; it was joined with the Congregational church in 1972 to become the United Reformed Church of Redhill. Another modern church, this was built in 1902. The war memorial is a bronze of a man holding a child in one arm and a torch in the other.

◆

REDHILL
St Paul's Church c1965
At this time there were several more years before the amalgamation with the Congregational church. The whole view is instantly recognisable today.

REDHILL, ST PAUL'S CHURCH C1965 R17088

REDHILL
St John's Church c1965

Built to the south of the town in 1843, St John's was soon considered too small for its purpose, and a rebuild was started in 1889. It stands today substantially as it was then. The pub in the foreground is now The Earlswood Arms.

◆

REDHILL
Holy Trinity Church c1965

This is a remarkably modern-looking church, considering that it was built in 1907. There are few change to see here; a brick wall replaces the hedge and fence, and the crosses over the porch and higher roof have gone.

REDHILL, ST JOHN'S CHURCH C1965 R17034

REDHILL, HOLY TRINITY CHURCH C1965 R17072

REDHILL
Redstone Hill 1906 54748
This is the main road leading away to the east. The houses to the right can still be seen, although trees in the garden hide them from the road to some degree. The extreme right-hand house is now a guest house colourwashed mint-green.

REDHILL
St Anne's Walk 1909
Here we see a pretty area of the town close to St. Anne's School, where a small brook flows. Perhaps the young man is sitting contemplating whether or not to jump in the water on what appears to be a lovely sunny day.

◆

REDHILL
The Colman Institute 1906
This peaceful scene is on a tree-lined London Road: this was before it became the busy A23, the main highway between London and Brighton. The sports and games fields, together with the Colman Institute, are no more.

REDHILL, ST ANNE'S WALK 1909 61884

REDHILL, THE COLMAN INSTITUTE 1906 56215

REDHILL, THE MONSON ARMS c1965 R17039
A fine example of a post-war pub, the Monson Arms - named after a local nobleman- advertises Double Diamond, a real name from the past, and has children sitting outside rather than in the bar as is so often the case today. A Wolseley and a Ford Zodiac adorn the car park.

REDHILL, THE MARKET HALL 1899 43148
The Market Hall, on the corner of London and Station Road, was opened in 1861; it was a financial disaster at first. The local council met there, and eventually a livestock market was started opposite. This changed the fortunes of the Hall. By the time our photographer visited, a west wing (the section to the left) had been added.

REDHILL, THE MARKET HALL 1915 67817

Now an east wing has been added. This took place in 1904. The left-hand side of the building is being used by the London & South Western Bank Ltd, established in 1862. They were taken over by Barclays in the 1920s. Also within the complex was the post office, the county court, the Literary Institute and a stage with a dance floor.

REDHILL, THE MARKET HALL 1933 85481

By now, entertainment was the main use for this building. Up-and-coming names would appear there in the 1950s, including Petula Clark and Kenny Ball. It was demolished in 1982, and the Harlequin Theatre was built on the site.

REDHILL, 1908 59628

Fashions are to the fore in this most attractive picture. The two ladies are fairly young, and could well be nannies looking after the children in the foreground. Often, uniforms were provided for women undertaking that task, but not always. Do we have an exception here? Reigate and Redhill Hospital can be seen in the background.

REDHILL
The Hospital 1908 59627
Reigate and Redhill Hospital was founded around
1860. We see the strange sight of a young man
pushing a perambulator to the door, there to be
greeted by a nurse. A dog is tied to the fence to the
right of the gate.

REDHILL
Linkfield Corner 1928 80969
With care, you will still identify this location. The YMCA building (centre distance) has disappeared to make way for a roundabout. The fishmongers is a Chinese takeaway; the row of shops to the right are still there, albeit with different occupants. You can even catch a bus at the same place - directly behind the left-hand vehicle.

REDHILL, LONDON ROAD c1955 R17003

This view gives an indication of how complete the destruction of central Redhill has been. The scene is no more. Much of the street to the extreme right - Clarenden Road - is now part of Queensway; the Harlequin Complex and Sainsbury's occupy much of this area.

REDHILL, LONDON ROAD c1965 R17093

By the time of this photograph, the traffic that would prove the undoing of Redhill is beginning to create problems. The cars in shot almost make up a hit parade of English motor memories: Austin, 1100, Singer Vogue, Hillman Minx, Vauxhall Victor, Triumph Herald and an assortment of Fords. It is amazing that one building in this view remains: the post office, the one with telephone boxes outside, but not used as such today.

REDHILL
London Road c1965

Another building to bite the dust in the 1980s was the vast emporium - the one with the blinds down. The South Suburban Co-operative Society operated this place, built in the immediate pre-war years. The original Co-op here was the Reigate Industrial and Providential Society from 1861. They opened their first shop in Redhill in 1898.

◆

REDHILL
Garlands Road 1906

This view looks down Brighton Road towards the town centre, with Garland Road to the left. The New Inn, although still intact and quite recognisable as an old pub, is now a plumbing and bathroom centre.

REDHILL, LONDON ROAD c1965 R17090A

REDHILL, GARLANDS ROAD 1906 55044

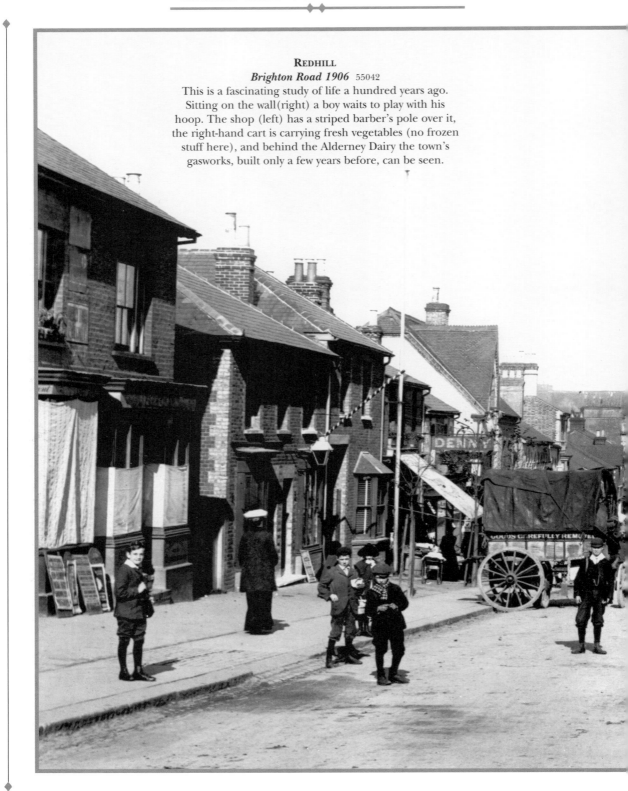

REDHILL
Brighton Road 1906 55042
This is a fascinating study of life a hundred years ago.
Sitting on the wall (right) a boy waits to play with his
hoop. The shop (left) has a striped barber's pole over it,
the right-hand cart is carrying fresh vegetables (no frozen
stuff here), and behind the Alderney Dairy the town's
gasworks, built only a few years before, can be seen.

REDHILL, BRIGHTON ROAD 1906 55041
Almost a century later, this view is just recognisable. The Noah's Ark pub on the right was eventually demolished after a period of other business usage, and replaced with flats. For the rest, apart from road widening, we now have odd shops, office blocks and spare ground.

REDHILL, BRIGHTON ROAD 1915 67829
We are still on Brighton Road, but much further south than photograph No 55042 and taken almost a decade later. The omnibus has 'Reigate' on its destination board: it will descend into town to pick up more passengers before heading west. The trees on the left, so much more mature here, have all now been removed: in the interests of road safety!

REDHILL, BRIGHTON ROAD 1915 67828

A large percentage of the people in this photograph are soldiers. But it was right in the middle of the 1914-18 war. Are they waiting for the pub to open? There seems to be a lot of litter blowing about the streets, and horse manure is plainly visible.

REDHILL, BRIGHTON ROAD c1955 R17026

The roadside trees have now gone. The column outside the pub was a police telephone. In the days before personal radios, officers on foot (remember them?) would be scheduled to visit this spot at given times - to 'make a point' - so that messages could be relayed. In the distance, the Redhill to Reading railway bridge and the spire of St Joseph's can be seen.

REDHILL

High Street 1906 55035

The High Street is now pedestrianised for much of its length. Today, on the left is the Belfry Centre. The taller building in the distance is the first marker today: a Firlot and Firkin pub. There is also a Lloyds Bank. Note the small cart to the left, a milk retailer. Alongside is a huge display of footwear. Maypole Dairy, International Stores and Express Tea are now merely memories.

REDHILL, STATION ROAD 1906 55033

As we look south along Station Road, one name jumps out after almost a century of trading: J Sainsbury. Today, apart from the railway, the view is completely gone. There are now offices to the left and new shops to the right. Sainsbury's new mega-store is a few yards to the north.

REDHILL, HIGH STREET 1933 85482

The street is a little more built-up than in the 1906 views. On the extreme left is a branch of Woolworth's. Although in a much newer building, the company still trade from this site. Next door, radios are advertised for sale. At this time, they were still not an item found in every household.

REDHILL, HIGH STREET 1933 85483

Most of this series of photographs were taken within a few yards of each other. In this instance, the camera is pointing north. The cinema on the left is showing 'Love me Tonight', a 1932 movie starring Maurice Chevalier and Jeanette MacDonald; she would later partner Nelson Eddy in a series of memorable musicals. This film has been described as 'the most fluently cinematic comedy musical ever made'.

REDHILL, HIGH STREET 1933 85484

The Tower pub can still be seen today. Re-named The Dog and Duck, the ground floor stone facing has been replaced by timber. Shops still line the right-hand side, but they are all new.

REDHILL, HIGH STREET C1955 R17008

It is twenty years and a war after photograph No 85484, and not much has changed. Street lighting has been improved, and there is a pedestrian crossing indicated by Belisha beacons. These were the fore-runners of zebra crossings: the road surface was clearly marked, and the amber globes flashed rather than showed a continuous light.

REDHILL, LONDON ROAD 1936 87305

It is all change again here. Barclays Bank has disappeared, and the Quadrant Shopping Centre has grown in its place. Across the road, the Baptist church that was built in 1866 has given way to Boots Opticians. The Baptists moved to a new, quieter site on Hatchlands Road in 1959.

REDHILL, HIGH STREET c1955 R17007

Here we see Burton's the Tailor's, which was in the distance in photograph No 87305. A police telephone similar to the one we saw earlier is outside. The phrase 'full Monty' is ascribed by some to this shop. In the immediate post-war years, it was used to identify a three-piece suit (one with waistcoat as opposed to just trousers and jacket), supplied by the company Montague Burton.

REDHILL, HIGH STREET c1955 R17302

There are commercial vehicles aplenty here. The one on the right appears to be an 'O' model Bedford articulated unit. The traffic, though, has grown appreciably. It would continue to multiply until the street was pedestrianised and sanity returned.

REDHILL, HIGH STREET C1965 R17052

As we look south again, some of the shop names now become more familiar. To the left, Dewhurst's are just beyond Fine Fare, and Freeman Hardy and Willis is on the right. Most of this is now gone. A British Road Services delivery truck is off-loading at one of the shops.

REDHILL, HIGH STREET C1965 R17054

We are back outside the Tower - soon to be The Dog and Duck. The crossing has now transmogrified into a zebra variety. On the left, offices replace all the buildings as far as the square office block.

REDHILL
St Anne's School 1886

A classic piece of Victorian extravaganza, St Anne's School was a combined chapel, foundlings school and home to the St Anne's Society. Of red brick construction, the whole building survived until well after the last war.

◆

REDHILL
Earlswood Lake c1955

There are two lakes at Earlswood. Boating is the pastime here, with a wonderful assortment of craft and forms of propulsion. Boat No 3 is propelled by hand-wound paddles, the two boats at either side of the picture by oars, and the central trip boat by outboard motor. These were still in their infancy in those days, and could be gloriously temperamental.

REDHILL, ST ANNE'S SCHOOL 1886 18928A

REDHILL, EARLSWOOD LAKE c1955 R17301

REDHILL, EARLSWOOD LAKE c1955 R17303
It is standing room only in this busy scene at the pool. Although the water looks shallow, there must be a deeper section, or the diving platform would not be of much use.

REDHILL, THE TECHNICAL INSTITUTE 1906 55040
At the time this picture was taken, this building was the Redhill Technical Institute School of Art. It held day and evening classes in art, science and technology. It was in use until the end of the 1960s and was finally demolished in the mid 1990s.

Index

Frith Book Co Titles

www.francisfrith.co.uk

The Frith Book Company publishes over 100 new titles each year. A selection of those currently available are listed below. For latest catalogue please contact Frith Book Co.

Town Books 96 pages, approx 100 photos. County and Themed Books 128 pages, approx 150 photos (unless specified). All titles hardback laminated case and jacket except those indicated pb (paperback)

Amersham, Chesham & Rickmansworth (pb)			Derby (pb)	1-85937-367-4	£9.99
	1-85937-340-2	£9.99	Derbyshire (pb)	1-85937-196-5	£9.99
Ancient Monuments & Stone Circles	1-85937-143-4	£17.99	Devon (pb)	1-85937-297-x	£9.99
Aylesbury (pb)	1-85937-227-9	£9.99	Dorset (pb)	1-85937-269-4	£9.99
Bakewell	1-85937-113-2	£12.99	Dorset Churches	1-85937-172-8	£17.99
Barnstaple (pb)	1-85937-300-3	£9.99	Dorset Coast (pb)	1-85937-299-6	£9.99
Bath (pb)	1-85937419-0	£9.99	Dorset Living Memories	1-85937-210-4	£14.99
Bedford (pb)	1-85937-205-8	£9.99	Down the Severn	1-85937-118-3	£14.99
Berkshire (pb)	1-85937-191-4	£9.99	Down the Thames (pb)	1-85937-278-3	£9.99
Berkshire Churches	1-85937-170-1	£17.99	Down the Trent	1-85937-311-9	£14.99
Blackpool (pb)	1-85937-382-8	£9.99	Dublin (pb)	1-85937-231-7	£9.99
Bognor Regis (pb)	1-85937-431-x	£9.99	East Anglia (pb)	1-85937-265-1	£9.99
Bournemouth	1-85937-067-5	£12.99	East London	1-85937-080-2	£14.99
Bradford (pb)	1-85937-204-x	£9.99	East Sussex	1-85937-130-2	£14.99
Brighton & Hove(pb)	1-85937-192-2	£8.99	Eastbourne	1-85937-061-6	£12.99
Bristol (pb)	1-85937-264-3	£9.99	Edinburgh (pb)	1-85937-193-0	£8.99
British Life A Century Ago (pb)	1-85937-213-9	£9.99	England in the 1880s	1-85937-331-3	£17.99
Buckinghamshire (pb)	1-85937-200-7	£9.99	English Castles (pb)	1-85937-434-4	£9.99
Camberley (pb)	1-85937-222-8	£9.99	English Country Houses	1-85937-161-2	£17.99
Cambridge (pb)	1-85937-422-0	£9.99	Essex (pb)	1-85937-270-8	£9.99
Cambridgeshire (pb)	1-85937-420-4	£9.99	Exeter	1-85937-126-4	£12.99
Canals & Waterways (pb)	1-85937-291-0	£9.99	Exmoor	1-85937-132-9	£14.99
Canterbury Cathedral (pb)	1-85937-179-5	£9.99	Falmouth	1-85937-066-7	£12.99
Cardiff (pb)	1-85937-093-4	£9.99	Folkestone (pb)	1-85937-124-8	£9.99
Carmarthenshire	1-85937-216-3	£14.99	Glasgow (pb)	1-85937-190-6	£9.99
Chelmsford (pb)	1-85937-310-0	£9.99	Gloucestershire	1-85937-102-7	£14.99
Cheltenham (pb)	1-85937-095-0	£9.99	Great Yarmouth (pb)	1-85937-426-3	£9.99
Cheshire (pb)	1-85937-271-6	£9.99	Greater Manchester (pb)	1-85937-266-x	£9.99
Chester	1-85937-090-x	£12.99	Guildford (pb)	1-85937-410-7	£9.99
Chesterfield	1-85937-378-x	£9.99	Hampshire (pb)	1-85937-279-1	£9.99
Chichester (pb)	1-85937-228-7	£9.99	Hampshire Churches (pb)	1-85937-207-4	£9.99
Colchester (pb)	1-85937-188-4	£8.99	Harrogate	1-85937-423-9	£9.99
Cornish Coast	1-85937-163-9	£14.99	Hastings & Bexhill (pb)	1-85937-131-0	£9.99
Cornwall (pb)	1-85937-229-5	£9.99	Heart of Lancashire (pb)	1-85937-197-3	£9.99
Cornwall Living Memories	1-85937-248-1	£14.99	Helston (pb)	1-85937-214-7	£9.99
Cotswolds (pb)	1-85937-230-9	£9.99	Hereford (pb)	1-85937-175-2	£9.99
Cotswolds Living Memories	1-85937-255-4	£14.99	Herefordshire	1-85937-174-4	£14.99
County Durham	1-85937-123-x	£14.99	Hertfordshire (pb)	1-85937-247-3	£9.99
Croydon Living Memories	1-85937-162-0	£9.99	Horsham (pb)	1-85937-432-8	£9.99
Cumbria	1-85937-101-9	£14.99	Humberside	1-85937-215-5	£14.99
Dartmoor	1-85937-145-0	£14.99	Hythe, Romney Marsh & Ashford	1-85937-256-2	£9.99

Available from your local bookshop or from the publisher

Frith Book Co Titles (continued)

Title	ISBN	Price	Title	ISBN	Price
Ipswich (pb)	1-85937-424-7	£9.99	St Ives (pb)	1-85937415-8	£9.99
Ireland (pb)	1-85937-181-7	£9.99	Scotland (pb)	1-85937-182-5	£9.99
Isle of Man (pb)	1-85937-268-6	£9.99	Scottish Castles (pb)	1-85937-323-2	£9.99
Isles of Scilly	1-85937-136-1	£14.99	Sevenoaks & Tunbridge	1-85937-057-8	£12.99
Isle of Wight (pb)	1-85937-429-8	£9.99	Sheffield, South Yorks (pb)	1-85937-267-8	£9.99
Isle of Wight Living Memories	1-85937-304-6	£14.99	Shrewsbury (pb)	1-85937-325-9	£9.99
Kent (pb)	1-85937-189-2	£9.99	Shropshire (pb)	1-85937-326-7	£9.99
Kent Living Memories	1-85937-125-6	£14.99	Somerset	1-85937-153-1	£14.99
Lake District (pb)	1-85937-275-9	£9.99	South Devon Coast	1-85937-107-8	£14.99
Lancaster, Morecambe & Heysham (pb)	1-85937-233-3	£9.99	South Devon Living Memories	1-85937-168-x	£14.99
Leeds (pb)	1-85937-202-3	£9.99	South Hams	1-85937-220-1	£14.99
Leicester	1-85937-073-x	£12.99	Southampton (pb)	1-85937-427-1	£9.99
Leicestershire (pb)	1-85937-185-x	£9.99	Southport (pb)	1-85937-425-5	£9.99
Lincolnshire (pb)	1-85937-433-6	£9.99	Staffordshire	1-85937-047-0	£12.99
Liverpool & Merseyside (pb)	1-85937-234-1	£9.99	Stratford upon Avon	1-85937-098-5	£12.99
London (pb)	1-85937-183-3	£9.99	Suffolk (pb)	1-85937-221-x	£9.99
Ludlow (pb)	1-85937-176-0	£9.99	Suffolk Coast	1-85937-259-7	£14.99
Luton (pb)	1-85937-235-x	£9.99	Surrey (pb)	1-85937-240-6	£9.99
Maidstone	1-85937-056-x	£14.99	Sussex (pb)	1-85937-184-1	£9.99
Manchester (pb)	1-85937-198-1	£9.99	Swansea (pb)	1-85937-167-1	£9.99
Middlesex	1-85937-158-2	£14.99	Tees Valley & Cleveland	1-85937-211-2	£14.99
New Forest	1-85937-128-0	£14.99	Thanet (pb)	1-85937-116-7	£9.99
Newark (pb)	1-85937-366-6	£9.99	Tiverton (pb)	1-85937-178-7	£9.99
Newport, Wales (pb)	1-85937-258-9	£9.99	Torbay	1-85937-063-2	£12.99
Newquay (pb)	1-85937-421-2	£9.99	Truro	1-85937-147-7	£12.99
Norfolk (pb)	1-85937-195-7	£9.99	Victorian and Edwardian Cornwall	1-85937-252-x	£14.99
Norfolk Living Memories	1-85937-217-1	£14.99	Victorian & Edwardian Devon	1-85937-253-8	£14.99
Northamptonshire	1-85937-150-7	£14.99	Victorian & Edwardian Kent	1-85937-149-3	£14.99
Northumberland Tyne & Wear (pb)	1-85937-281-3	£9.99	Vic & Ed Maritime Album	1-85937-144-2	£17.99
North Devon Coast	1-85937-146-9	£14.99	Victorian and Edwardian Sussex	1-85937-157-4	£14.99
North Devon Living Memories	1-85937-261-9	£14.99	Victorian & Edwardian Yorkshire	1-85937-154-x	£14.99
North London	1-85937-206-6	£14.99	Victorian Seaside	1-85937-159-0	£17.99
North Wales (pb)	1-85937-298-8	£9.99	Villages of Devon (pb)	1-85937-293-7	£9.99
North Yorkshire (pb)	1-85937-236-8	£9.99	Villages of Kent (pb)	1-85937-294-5	£9.99
Norwich (pb)	1-85937-194-9	£8.99	Villages of Sussex (pb)	1-85937-295-3	£9.99
Nottingham (pb)	1-85937-324-0	£9.99	Warwickshire (pb)	1-85937-203-1	£9.99
Nottinghamshire (pb)	1-85937-187-6	£9.99	Welsh Castles (pb)	1-85937-322-4	£9.99
Oxford (pb)	1-85937-411-5	£9.99	West Midlands (pb)	1-85937-289-9	£9.99
Oxfordshire (pb)	1-85937-430-1	£9.99	West Sussex	1-85937-148-5	£14.99
Peak District (pb)	1-85937-280-5	£9.99	West Yorkshire (pb)	1-85937-201-5	£9.99
Penzance	1-85937-069-1	£12.99	Weymouth (pb)	1-85937-209-0	£9.99
Peterborough (pb)	1-85937-219-8	£9.99	Wiltshire (pb)	1-85937-277-5	£9.99
Piers	1-85937-237-6	£17.99	Wiltshire Churches (pb)	1-85937-171-x	£9.99
Plymouth	1-85937-119-1	£12.99	Wiltshire Living Memories	1-85937-245-7	£14.99
Poole & Sandbanks (pb)	1-85937-251-1	£9.99	Winchester (pb)	1-85937-428-x	£9.99
Preston (pb)	1-85937-212-0	£9.99	Windmills & Watermills	1-85937-242-2	£17.99
Reading (pb)	1-85937-238-4	£9.99	Worcester (pb)	1-85937-165-5	£9.99
Romford (pb)	1-85937-319-4	£9.99	Worcestershire	1-85937-152-3	£14.99
Salisbury (pb)	1-85937-239-2	£9.99	York (pb)	1-85937-199-x	£9.99
Scarborough (pb)	1-85937-379-8	£9.99	Yorkshire (pb)	1-85937-186-8	£9.99
St Albans (pb)	1-85937-341-0	£9.99	Yorkshire Living Memories	1-85937-166-3	£14.99

See Frith books on the internet www.francisfrith.co.uk

FRITH PRODUCTS & SERVICES

Francis Frith would doubtless be pleased to know that the pioneering publishing venture he started in 1860 still continues today. A hundred and forty years later, The Francis Frith Collection continues in the same innovative tradition and is now one of the foremost publishers of vintage photographs in the world. Some of the current activities include:

Interior Decoration

Today Frith's photographs can be seen framed and as giant wall murals in thousands of pubs, restaurants, hotels, banks, retail stores and other public buildings throughout the country. In every case they enhance the unique local atmosphere of the places they depict and provide reminders of gentler days in an increasingly busy and frenetic world.

Product Promotions

Frith products are used by many major companies to promote the sales of their own products or to reinforce their own history and heritage. Frith promotions have been used by Hovis bread, Courage beers, Scots Porage Oats, Colman's mustard, Cadbury's foods, Mellow Birds coffee, Dunhill pipe tobacco, Guinness, and Bulmer's Cider.

Genealogy and Family History

As the interest in family history and roots grows world-wide, more and more people are turning to Frith's photographs of Great Britain for images of the towns, villages and streets where their ancestors lived; and, of course, photographs of the churches and chapels where their ancestors were christened, married and buried are an essential part of every genealogy tree and family album.

Frith Products

All Frith photographs are available Framed or just as Mounted Prints and Posters (size 23 x 16 inches). These may be ordered from the address below. From time to time other products - Address Books, Calendars, Table Mats, etc - are available.

The Internet

Already twenty thousand Frith photographs can be viewed and purchased on the internet through the Frith websites and a myriad of partner sites.

For more detailed information on Frith companies and products, look at these sites:

www.francisfrith.co.uk
www.francisfrith.com
(for North American visitors)

See the complete list of Frith Books at:

www.francisfrith.co.uk

This web site is regularly updated with the latest list of publications from the Frith Book Company. If you wish to buy books relating to another part of the country that your local bookshop does not stock, you may purchase on-line.

For further information, trade, or author enquiries please contact us at the address below:
The Francis Frith Collection, Frith's Barn, Teffont, Salisbury, Wiltshire, England SP3 5QP.
Tel: +44 (0)1722 716 376 Fax: +44 (0)1722 716 881 Email: sales@francisfrith.co.uk

See Frith books on the internet www.francisfrith.co.uk

TO RECEIVE YOUR **FREE** MOUNTED PRINT

Mounted Print
Overall size 14 x 11 inches

Cut out this Voucher and return it with your remittance for £1.95 to cover postage and handling, to UK addresses. For overseas addresses please include £4.00 post and handling. Choose any photograph included in this book. Your SEPIA print will be A4 in size, and mounted in a cream mount with burgundy rule line, overall size 14 x 11 inches.

Order additional Mounted Prints at HALF PRICE (only £7.49 each*)

If there are further pictures you would like to order, possibly as gifts for friends and family, purchase them at half price (no additional postage and handling required).

Have your Mounted Prints framed*

For an additional £14.95 per print you can have your chosen Mounted Print framed in an elegant polished wood and gilt moulding, overall size 16 x 13 inches (no additional postage and handling required).

> *** IMPORTANT!**
> **These special prices are only available if ordered using the original voucher on this page (no copies permitted) and at the same time as your free Mounted Print, for delivery to the same address**

Frith Collectors' Guild

From time to time we publish a magazine of news and stories about Frith photographs and further special offers of Frith products. If you would like 12 months FREE membership, please return this form.

Send completed forms to:
The Francis Frith Collection, Frith's Barn, Teffont, Salisbury, Wiltshire SP3 5QP

Voucher for **FREE** and Reduced Price Frith Prints

Picture no.	Page number	Qty	Mounted @ £7.49	Framed + £14.95	Total Cost
		1	**Free of charge***	£	£
			£7.49	£	£
			£7.49	£	£
			£7.49	£	£
			£7.49	£	£
			£7.49	£	£

Please allow 28 days for delivery   *** Post & handling**   **£1.95**

Book Title . . . .   **Total Order Cost**   **£**

Please do not photocopy this voucher. Only the original is valid, so please cut it out and return it to us.

I enclose a cheque / postal order for £ . . . .
made payable to 'The Francis Frith Collection'
OR please debit my Mastercard / Visa / Switch / Amex card
(credit cards please on all overseas orders)

Number . . . .

Issue No(Switch only) . . . . .Valid from (Amex/Switch) . . . .

Expires . . . . Signature . . . .

Name   Mr/Mrs/Ms . . . .

Address . . . .

. . . .

. . . . Postcode . . . .

Daytime Tel No . . . .   Valid to 31/12/03

The Francis Frith Collectors' Guild

Please enrol me as a member for 12 months free of charge.

Name   Mr/Mrs/Ms . . . .

Address . . . .

. . . .

. . . .

. . . . Postcode . . . .

Would you like to find out more about Francis Frith?

We have recently recruited some entertaining speakers who are happy to visit local groups, clubs and societies to give an illustrated talk documenting Frith's travels and photographs. If you are a member of such a group and are interested in hosting a presentation, we would love to hear from you.

Our speakers bring with them a small selection of our local town and county books, together with sample prints. They are happy to take orders. A small proportion of the order value is donated to the group who have hosted the presentation. The talks are therefore an excellent way of fundraising for small groups and societies.

Can you help us with information about any of the Frith photographs in this book?

We are gradually compiling an historical record for each of the photographs in the Frith archive. It is always fascinating to find out the names of the people shown in the pictures, as well as insights into the shops, buildings and other features depicted.

If you recognize anyone in the photographs in this book, or if you have information not already included in the author's caption, do let us know. We would love to hear from you, and will try to publish it in future books or articles.

Our production team

Frith books are produced by a small dedicated team at offices in the converted Grade II listed 18th-century barn at Teffont near Salisbury, illustrated above. Most have worked with the Frith Collection for many years. All have in common one quality: they have a passion for the Frith Collection. The team is constantly expanding, but currently includes:

Jason Buck, John Buck, Douglas Burns, Heather Crisp, Lucy Elcock, Isobel Hall, Rob Hames, Hazel Heaton, Peter Horne, James Kinnear, Tina Leary, Hannah Marsh, Eliza Sackett, Terence Sackett, Sandra Sanger, Lewis Taylor, Shelley Tolcher, Helen Vimpany, Clive Wathen and Jenny Wathen.